Vocabulary Skills, Grade 2

Contents

Vocabulary Skills, Grade 2, Introduction

One of the most basic elements of reading comprehension is understanding the meaning of words. However, students may not realize that they do not necessarily need to know the meaning of every word in a selection in order to understand what they are reading. They may be surprised to find that through reading, they can actually increase their knowledge of word meaning. The more words students know, the more they will be able to read, and conversely, the more they read, the more words they will know.

Students can use several strategies to help them determine the meaning of unfamiliar words they encounter while reading:
• using context clues
• analyzing prefixes, suffixes, and root words
• looking up unfamiliar words in the dictionary

Vocabulary Skills is designed to help students practice these strategies in order to incorporate them seamlessly into their approach to reading. New vocabulary words are introduced within the context of high-interest readings. Students can use these context clues to determine the meaning of unfamiliar words. Activities are designed to reinforce the use of all word meaning strategies.

By increasing their word power, students will also increase their scores on standardized tests.

Organization
The book is organized into five units, with five lessons in each unit. In Units 1–4, each lesson consists of a high-interest reading rich in context so that students can determine the meaning of the vocabulary words based on the context of the reading. Each lesson includes vocabulary activities and most contain a dictionary activity. The vocabulary activities include
• analogies,
• antonyms,
• base words,
• classifying,
• compound words,
• crossword puzzles,
• multiple meanings,
• synonyms,
• word groups,
• word puzzles, and
• word webs.

The dictionary skills include
• alphabetical order,
• guide words, and
• syllabication.

Each lesson provides a review of the vocabulary words, once again in a context-based approach, and gives students the chance to practice using the vocabulary words in their own original writing.

Unit 5 focuses on word analysis, with lessons dealing specifically with prefixes, suffixes, homophones, and words from other languages. The book concludes with a fun section so that students have the opportunity to play games with words.

Assessments
Vocabulary Skills uses two kinds of assessments:
• Two overall assessments located at the front of the book cover the new vocabulary words. One of these can be given as a pretest to gauge students' knowledge of the vocabulary. Later in the year, the other test can be administered to determine students' understanding, progress, and achievement.
• Each unit also has an assessment. These unit assessments can be administered at any time during the unit as a pretest, review, or posttest.

Vocabulary List
On page 3 is a list of all the vocabulary words contained in Units 1–4. You may want to distribute it to students so they will be able to incorporate the words into their writing for other assignments.

Correlation to Standards
The National Council of Teachers of English has stated in the "Standards for the English Language Arts" the following: "Students apply a wide range of strategies to comprehend, interpret, evaluate, and appreciate texts. They draw on their prior experience, their interaction with other readers and writers, their knowledge of word meaning and of other texts, their word identification strategies, and their understanding of textual features (e.g., sound-letter correspondence, sentence structure, context, graphics)." *Vocabulary Skills* helps students achieve this goal by providing strategies for students to comprehend what they read, increase their knowledge of word meaning, and expand their use of context clues.

Dictionaries and Other Reference Books
Students striving to increase their vocabulary benefit greatly from having access to dictionaries, thesauruses, and other books dealing with word meanings and origins. These resources should be readily available to students at all times.

Vocabulary List

amazing (9)
awful (4)

backyard (11)
bank (14)
barked (13)
basket (2)
behave (3)
brave (1)
broke (4)
brook (16)

chalk (4)
chimed (13)
comfortable (8)
couldn't (5)
court (2)

difficult (18)
dinner (10)
doghouse (11)
don't (5)
doorbell (20)
downstairs (1)
ducks (14)

early (7)
enemies (1)
everyone (20)
exploring (7)

farewell (8)
float (9)
fluffy (12)
foolish (3)
football (20)
fortunate (3)
forward (18)
frighten (3)
frowned (1)

gently (15)
giggle (3)
grin (10)

hiking (7)
hours (17)

insects (6)
inside (20)
isn't (5)
I've (5)

journey (8)

knocked (13)

large (9)
lean (7)
leaped (10)
listen (12)
luggage (8)

manners (15)
material (19)
meadow (16)
moon (9)
museum (17)

neighbor (12)
nervous (8)
newspaper (11)

ordered (15)
outside (11)

packed (6)
paintbrush (11)
paintings (16)
paws (15)
pieces (19)
playground (20)
puppy (12)
purred (13)

rainy (1)
rang (13)
remember (18)
reptiles (17)
restaurant (17)

safe (14)
scissors (19)
season (16)
sew (19)
shoot (2)
sidewalk (4)
sniff (14)
splashing (16)
stream (10)
stripes (19)
strong (7)
summer (9)
swing (2)

tag (14)
tangled (6)
teaching (18)
tent (10)
traveling (6)
treats (15)

umbrella (12)

wasn't (5)
watch (2)
week (17)
wings (6)
wondered (4)
wonderful (18)

Note: The numbers in parentheses refer to the lessons where the vocabulary words are taught.

Overall Assessment 1

Darken the letter of the word that fits best in the sentence.

1. A bird uses its _____ to fly.
- Ⓐ feathers
- Ⓑ beak
- Ⓒ wings

2. All _____ have six legs.
- Ⓐ animals
- Ⓑ insects
- Ⓒ inside

3. Margo was _____ by train to see her grandmother.
- Ⓐ tracking
- Ⓑ trucking
- Ⓒ traveling

4. They left _____ in the morning before the sun came up.
- Ⓐ early
- Ⓑ late
- Ⓒ forward

5. Tran likes to go _____ in the woods to look for animals.
- Ⓐ packing
- Ⓑ leading
- Ⓒ exploring

6. Dad has a _____ chair he likes to sleep in.
- Ⓐ comfortable
- Ⓑ painful
- Ⓒ sticky

7. Brad was so scared and _____ that he forgot what he was going to say.
- Ⓐ reminded
- Ⓑ nervous
- Ⓒ happy

8. The singer said _____ before getting in the car to leave.
- Ⓐ farewell
- Ⓑ hello
- Ⓒ greetings

9. We like to go swimming in the _____.
- Ⓐ winter
- Ⓑ fall
- Ⓒ summer

10. The _____ was a big ball in the night sky.
- Ⓐ sun
- Ⓑ moon
- Ⓒ flashlight

Overall Assessment 1, page 2

Darken the letter of the word that means the same, or about the same, as the boldfaced word.

11. packed **luggage**

Ⓐ rooms

Ⓑ lunches

Ⓒ bags

12. tangled in a net

Ⓐ jumping

Ⓑ swinging

Ⓒ stuck

13. a **brave** man

Ⓐ not scared

Ⓑ crying

Ⓒ funny

14. giggle out loud

Ⓐ read

Ⓑ yell

Ⓒ laugh

Darken the letter of the correct answer.

15. Choose the word that completes the sentence.

Jake bought ____ toy cars.

Ⓐ two

Ⓑ too

Ⓒ to

16. Choose the word that completes the sentence.

"Come ____ right now," said Mother.

Ⓐ her

Ⓑ hear

Ⓒ here

17. What is the prefix in the word unable?

Ⓐ un

Ⓑ ble

Ⓒ nab

18. What does the word rewrite mean?

Ⓐ do not write

Ⓑ write again

Ⓒ one who writes

19. Which word would be between the guide words cap and dog?

Ⓐ ducks

Ⓑ broke

Ⓒ court

Overall Assessment 2

Darken the letter of the word that fits best in the sentence.

1. Miguel planted a tree in the _____.
- Ⓐ building
- Ⓑ backyard
- Ⓒ bedroom

2. Mr. Jacobs hung the _____ in the hall.
- Ⓐ brook
- Ⓑ museum
- Ⓒ paintings

3. The children were wet after _____ in the water.
- Ⓐ splashing
- Ⓑ ducks
- Ⓒ downstairs

4. The movie was two _____ long.
- Ⓐ weeks
- Ⓑ hours
- Ⓒ seasons

5. Pam and Chou ate lunch in a _____.
- Ⓐ restaurant
- Ⓑ basket
- Ⓒ umbrella

6. Mrs. Oliver is _____ the puppy to come when his named is called.
- Ⓐ barking
- Ⓑ learning
- Ⓒ teaching

7. Ryan put the _____ of the puzzle together.
- Ⓐ pieces
- Ⓑ cuts
- Ⓒ stripes

8. Mother needs to _____ the button on Jack's coat.
- Ⓐ broke
- Ⓑ clean
- Ⓒ sew

9. Sonya rang the _____ when she got locked outside.
- Ⓐ doorbell
- Ⓑ doghouse
- Ⓒ football

10. The clock in the hall _____ the time.
- Ⓐ purred
- Ⓑ chimed
- Ⓒ knocked

Overall Assessment 2, page 2

Darken the letter of the word that means the same, or about the same, as the boldfaced word.

11. a **fluffy** blanket
- (A) hard
- (B) heavy
- (C) soft

12. listen to the music
- (A) hear
- (B) sing
- (C) clap

13. sniff a flower
- (A) see
- (B) smell
- (C) pick

14. pushed **gently**
- (A) roughly
- (B) carefully
- (C) quietly

Darken the letter of the correct answer.

15. Choose the word that completes the sentence.

Dad went _____ the store.
- (A) two
- (B) too
- (C) to

16. Choose the word that completes the sentence.

What movie did Ben go _____?
- (A) she
- (B) see
- (C) sea

17. What is the suffix in the word colorful?
- (A) co
- (B) lor
- (C) ful

18. What does the word quickly mean?
- (A) not quick
- (B) in a way that is quick
- (C) one who is quick

19. Which will come last if the words are listed in alphabetical order?
- (A) large
- (B) journey
- (C) manners

20. What is the prefix in the word unknown?
- (A) un
- (B) know
- (C) known

Unit 1 Assessment

Darken the letter of the word that fits best in the sentence.

1. Juan walked _____ to the bottom floor inside the store.
- Ⓐ upstairs
- Ⓑ downstairs
- Ⓒ outside

2. Mr. Han _____ when he saw the muddy shoes in the house.
- Ⓐ frowned
- Ⓑ smiled
- Ⓒ cheered

3. Sam took an umbrella because it was going to be a _____ day.
- Ⓐ sunny
- Ⓑ snowy
- Ⓒ rainy

4. Lisa was very _____ when she climbed the tree to save the kitten.
- Ⓐ brave
- Ⓑ hurt
- Ⓒ huge

5. Mrs. Butler looked at her _____ to check the time.
- Ⓐ bike
- Ⓑ watch
- Ⓒ hand

6. The chain on the park _____ was broken.
- Ⓐ slide
- Ⓑ seesaw
- Ⓒ swing

7. Sonya helped the team win when she threw the ball into the _____.
- Ⓐ basket
- Ⓑ bench
- Ⓒ home

8. The players ran up and down the _____ during the basketball game.
- Ⓐ field
- Ⓑ team
- Ⓒ court

9. A scary story can _____ small children.
- Ⓐ frighten
- Ⓑ carry
- Ⓒ waken

10. John was sent to his room when he did not _____ at dinner.
- Ⓐ laugh
- Ⓑ behave
- Ⓒ spill

Unit 1 Assessment, page 2

Darken the letter of the word that fits best in the sentence.

11. That funny joke made Leisha ____.

Ⓐ cry

Ⓑ run

Ⓒ giggle

12. Rita was ____ when she did not wear boots in the snow.

Ⓐ tired

Ⓑ foolish

Ⓒ smart

13. The glass ____ into pieces when it fell on the floor.

Ⓐ broke

Ⓑ rolled

Ⓒ drank

14. The teacher used ____ when she wrote on the board.

Ⓐ chalk

Ⓑ pencil

Ⓒ paint

15. A ____ is a safe place to walk.

Ⓐ lake

Ⓑ road

Ⓒ sidewalk

16. Kim took out the trash to get rid of the ____ smell.

Ⓐ sweet

Ⓑ awful

Ⓒ wonderful

17. Gina ____ why her father was not at the school to pick her up.

Ⓐ hoped

Ⓑ watered

Ⓒ wondered

18. The garden ____ very big.

Ⓐ wasn't

Ⓑ won't

Ⓒ can't

19. The children ____ hear their mother calling them.

Ⓐ couldn't

Ⓑ isn't

Ⓒ aren't

20. Hank ____ in the store.

Ⓐ don't

Ⓑ I've

Ⓒ wasn't

Name _____ Date _____

Making Friends

Read the story. Think about the meanings of the words in bold type.

Johnny Elton and I live in the same building. He lives **downstairs** below me. We used to be **enemies**. Johnny said he did not want to be friends with a girl. Whenever he saw me, he made a mean face and **frowned** at me. Then, one day we were waiting for the bus to go to school. It began to storm. Johnny got scared when he saw a flash of light in the **rainy** sky. I asked Johnny to stand under my umbrella. Then, we ran to a safe place to wait for the rain to stop. Johnny said I was **brave**. He says he likes people who are not afraid. Now, Johnny and I are friends. We play together all the time.

Look back at the words in bold type. Use clues in the story to figure out the meaning of each word. Write each word on the line next to its meaning.

_____ **1.** made an unhappy face by moving the eyebrows together

_____ **2.** not scared

_____ **3.** full of rain

_____ **4.** on a floor below

_____ **5.** not friends

Name _____ Date _____

Antonyms

Antonyms are words with opposite meanings.
EXAMPLES: big—small   long—short   up—down

Match the words in the box with their antonyms listed below. Write the words on the lines.

> brave   rainy   enemies   frowned   downstairs

_____ **1.** friends

_____ **2.** smiled

_____ **3.** scared

_____ **4.** sunny

_____ **5.** upstairs

Dictionary Skills

The words in a dictionary are listed in **ABC order**.
EXAMPLE: back, coat, door

Write the words in the box above in ABC order.
Write one word on each line.

1. _____

2. _____

3. _____

4. _____

5. _____

Name _____   Date _____

Word Wise

| brave | rainy | enemies | frowned | downstairs |

Choose the word from the box that makes sense in the sentences below.

1. Sara and her friends share an umbrella on

_____ days.

2. Dad _____ when he saw the clothes

on the floor.

3. The _____ man jumped into the water

to save the child.

4. Malika walked _____ to a store on the

first floor.

5. Jake does not have any _____ because

he is nice to everyone.

Writing

Write your own story about something that happened on a rainy day. Use as many words from the box as you can.

_____

_____

_____

_____

_____

Rita's Game

Read the story. Think about the meanings of the words in bold type.

I looked at my **watch** to see what time it was. I was late! My best friend Rita was playing in a ball game. I had told Rita that I would come to see the game. But I was late! I had taken my sister to the park to play on a **swing**. We needed to hurry to get to the basketball **court**. "Come on, Maria," I said. "We are going to miss Rita's game."

When I got to the court, I saw Rita grab the ball and **shoot**. The ball dropped through the **basket**. Rita had made the winning points! While I missed most of the game, I got to see the most important part of it. I got to see Rita smile.

Look back at the words in bold type. Use clues in the story to figure out the meaning of each word. Write each word on the line next to its meaning.

_____ **1.** to push something forward

_____ **2.** a seat held by ropes in which someone can move back and forth

_____ **3.** a metal circle with a net used in a basketball game

_____ **4.** a place where games are played

_____ **5.** something that measures time

Multiple Meanings

Some words have more than one meaning. You can use clues in the sentence to tell which meaning the word has.

EXAMPLE: leaves

meaning A: goes away. John **leaves** for camp next week.

meaning B: more than one leaf. Mom spent the morning raking **leaves**.

Write the letter of the correct meaning next to each sentence.

watch

meaning A: something that measures time

meaning B: to look at

_____ **1.** Did Jay watch television all day?

_____ **2.** Dan's watch showed the time to be two o'clock.

basket

meaning A: a metal circle with a net used in a basketball game

meaning B: something woven with straw or strips of wood that holds
things

_____ **3.** The ball missed the basket.

_____ **4.** Mother put the food in the basket.

swing

meaning A: a seat held by ropes in which
someone can move back and forth

meaning B: to move in a circle

_____ **5.** Baseball players swing a bat to hit the ball.

_____ **6.** Kevin has a swing in his backyard.

Word Wise

| shoot | swing | watch | court | basket |

Rewrite each sentence. Use one of the words from the box in place of a word or words in the sentence.

1. Mr. Edwards carefully pushed the baby on the seat held by ropes.

_____

2. The players will meet at the place to play a game after school.

_____

3. The crowd yelled happily when the ball went into the metal circle.

_____

4. Ed and Meiko come to the park to push forward the basketball.

_____

5. Jay bought a new something to measure time so that he would never be late again.

_____

Writing

Write your own story about a time you played in or watched a basketball game. Use as many words from the box as you can.

_____

_____

_____

_____

_____

A Dinosaur Dream

Read the story. Think about the meanings of the words in bold type.

I had a dream about a dinosaur. He was running after me. "Are you trying to **frighten** me?" I asked.

"Oh, I am so sorry," said the dinosaur. "I did not mean to scare you. I just want a friend."

"I'll be your friend," I said.

Then, the silly dinosaur made faces and jumped up and down. He looked so **foolish**. I began to **giggle**. "I will have to teach you how to **behave**," I said. "My mother will not let you in the house if you act silly."

"How **fortunate** that I met you!" the dinosaur said.

"Yes," I said. "We are lucky to be friends."

Look back at the words in bold type. Use clues in the story to figure out the meaning of each word. Write each word on the line next to its meaning.

_____ **1.** to laugh in a silly way

_____ **2.** to be lucky

_____ **3.** to make afraid

_____ **4.** to act in a good way

_____ **5.** silly

Synonyms

A **synonym** is a word that has the same, or almost the same, meaning as another word.
EXAMPLES: small—little   happy—glad

Write the letter of the synonym beside each word.

_____ **1.** foolish   A. scare

_____ **2.** behave   B. lucky

_____ **3.** giggle   C. laugh

_____ **4.** frighten   D. silly

_____ **5.** fortunate   E. act nicely

Dictionary Skills

 Guide words are two words at the top of each dictionary page. Guide words tell the first and last entry words on the page. All the words are in ABC order.
EXAMPLE:
Guide words: **note**   **time**
Entry words on page: pie,   red,   sip

Darken the circle for the correct answer.

1. Which word would be between the guide words <u>ball</u> and <u>goat</u>?
   Ⓐ foolish   Ⓑ apple   Ⓒ hat

2. Which word would be between the guide words <u>egg</u> and <u>jar</u>?
   Ⓐ lap   Ⓑ dig   Ⓒ giggle

Word Wise

| giggle | foolish | behave | frighten | fortunate |

Choose the word from the box that makes sense in the sentences below.

1. Tina was _____ to find her

lost dog.

2. The joke made me _____ out loud.

3. We always _____ and talk quietly in the

library.

4. Nick looked _____ when he stuck his fingers

in his ears.

5. Wendy jumped out from behind the tree to

_____ her brother.

Writing

Write your own story about a dream you had. Use as many words from the box as you can.

_____

_____

_____

_____

_____

_____

The Break Up

Read the words written in a diary. Think about the meanings of the words in bold type.

Dear Diary,

Today I went to Mike's house. We were playing with toy cars. I pushed one car too hard. It rolled into a wall and **broke**. Mike got so angry. He told me to leave.

I felt **awful**. I did not mean to break his toy. I wanted to tell Mike that I was sorry. So I got some **chalk**. I drew a clown face on the **sidewalk** beside his house. I **wondered** if Mike and I would make up. It just was not much fun playing alone. Soon, the door opened. Mike came out. He looked sad, too. Mike and I said that we were sorry at the same time. I'm glad that we are friends again.

Beth

Look back at the words in bold type. Use clues in the diary to figure out the meaning of each word. Write each word on the line next to its meaning.

_____ **1.** very bad

_____ **2.** something to draw with

_____ **3.** a place to walk beside a street

_____ **4.** came apart

_____ **5.** wanted to know or learn

Word Groups

Words can be grouped by how they are alike.

EXAMPLE: types of toys: dolls, cars, balls

Read each group of words. Think about how they are alike. Write the word from the box that best completes each group.

chalk	broke	awful	wondered	sidewalk

1. smashed, ripped, _____

2. paint, crayon, _____

3. trail, track, _____

4. bad, terrible, _____

5. hoped, questioned, _____

Dictionary Skills

The words in a dictionary are listed in **ABC order**.

EXAMPLE: back, coat, door

Write the words in the box above in ABC order. Write one word on each line.

1. _____

2. _____

3. _____

4. _____

5. _____

Word Wise

chalk   broke   awful   wondered   sidewalk

Choose the word from the box that makes sense in the sentences below.

1. Max _____ which car he

should buy for his brother.

2. Amy rode her bike down the _____.

3. Greg drew a picture with some _____.

4. The vase fell off the table and _____

into pieces.

5. Harry felt _____ when he made his sister cry.

Writing

Write your own story about a time a friend got angry with you. Use as many words from the box as you can.

_____

_____

_____

_____

_____

_____

_____

Name _____ Date _____

A Lost Friend

Read the story. Think about the meanings of the words in bold type.

Milly had something she wanted to show her friend Beth. So, Milly went to Beth's house.

"She **isn't** in the house," said Mrs. Ford. "Try looking in the backyard."

So Milly looked outside. But Beth **wasn't** there, either.

"I **don't** know where Beth could be," thought Milly on her way home. Milly **couldn't** have been more surprised to see Beth waiting for her when she got home.

"**I've** been looking for you!" exclaimed Milly. "I want you to see my new pet turtle."

Look back at the words in bold type. Use clues in the story to figure out the meaning of each word. Write each word on the line next to its meaning.

_____ **1.** was not

_____ **2.** I have

_____ **3.** is not

_____ **4.** do not

_____ **5.** could not

Contractions

A **contraction** is a way to put two words together. An **apostrophe** (') takes the place of one or more letters.

EXAMPLES:

are + not = aren't

let + us = let's

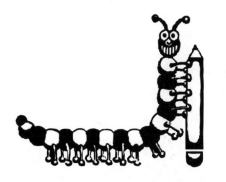

Write each contraction. Then, use each contraction in a sentence.

1. is + not = _____

_____

2. could + not = _____

_____

3. I + have = _____

_____

4. do + not = _____

_____

5. was + not = _____

_____

Name _____ Date _____

Word Wise

I've   isn't   don't   wasn't   couldn't

Rewrite each sentence. Use one of the words from the box in place of a word or some words in the sentence.

1. The boys do not want to go to the park.

_____

2. Dana could not wait to eat dinner.

_____

3. I have read that book already.

_____

4. Pam is not going to ride the bus today.

_____

5. The dog was not in the backyard.

_____

Writing

Write your own story about a time you were looking for someone or something. Use as many words from the box as you can.

_____

_____

_____

_____

_____

Unit 2 Assessment

Darken the letter of the word that means the same, or about the same, as the boldfaced word.

1. **packed** a bag
   - Ⓐ filled
   - Ⓑ carried
   - Ⓒ bought

2. flying **insects**
   - Ⓐ birds
   - Ⓑ planes
   - Ⓒ bugs

3. **traveling** in a car
   - Ⓐ sleeping
   - Ⓑ going
   - Ⓒ working

4. **tangled** in a net
   - Ⓐ caught
   - Ⓑ swimming
   - Ⓒ found

5. **wings** of a bird
   - Ⓐ hearing parts
   - Ⓑ seeing parts
   - Ⓒ flying parts

6. **hiking** in the woods
   - Ⓐ driving
   - Ⓑ walking
   - Ⓒ cooking

7. **early** in the morning
   - Ⓐ near the beginning
   - Ⓑ near the middle
   - Ⓒ near the end

8. **exploring** a house
   - Ⓐ cleaning
   - Ⓑ looking in
   - Ⓒ building

9. **lean** against a tree
   - Ⓐ rest
   - Ⓑ cut
   - Ⓒ plant

10. load the **luggage**
    - Ⓐ buses
    - Ⓑ boxes
    - Ⓒ bags

Unit 2 Assessment, page 2

Darken the letter of the word that means the same, or about the same, as the boldfaced word.

11. a long **journey**
- Ⓐ laugh
- Ⓑ road
- Ⓒ trip

12. feeling **nervous**
- Ⓐ worried
- Ⓑ happy
- Ⓒ angry

13. saying **farewell**
- Ⓐ come in
- Ⓑ hello
- Ⓒ good-bye

14. a **comfortable** bed
- Ⓐ messy
- Ⓑ feeling good
- Ⓒ tired

15. an **amazing** baby
- Ⓐ cute
- Ⓑ surprising
- Ⓒ small

16. a **large** dog
- Ⓐ big
- Ⓑ fluffy
- Ⓒ noisy

17. leaped into the water
- Ⓐ pushed
- Ⓑ swam
- Ⓒ jumped

18. gave a **grin**
- Ⓐ hug
- Ⓑ gift
- Ⓒ smile

19. fixed **dinner**
- Ⓐ supper
- Ⓑ dolls
- Ⓒ cars

20. crossed a **stream**
- Ⓐ finger
- Ⓑ bridge
- Ⓒ water

Trudy's Trip

Read the story. Think about the meanings of the words in bold type.

Trudy was looking forward to the family trip. They were **traveling** to a place that was the home of a special butterfly. Trudy could hardly wait. She loved learning about **insects**. She **packed** her bug book and net in her bag. The net would help her get a closer look at a butterfly. Trudy knew she had to be careful when she used the net. The **wings** of the

butterfly could get stuck in the net. A butterfly that got **tangled** could get hurt. Trudy knew that she would have to be very careful to free the butterfly after she looked at it.

Look back at the words in bold type. Use clues in the story to figure out the meaning of each word. Write each word on the line next to its meaning.

_____ **1.** going from one place to another

_____ **2.** twisted together; stuck

_____ **3.** filled up with things

_____ **4.** the parts that help something fly

_____ **5.** small animals with six legs

Base Words

Base words are words without any endings or other word parts added to them. Some endings are **s**, **ed**, and **ing**. Sometimes the spelling of the base word changes when an ending is added to it.

EXAMPLES: net   nets

open   opened

love   loved

look   looking

Write the base word of each word below. Then, use the base word in a sentence.

1. wings _____

_____

2. tangled _____

_____

3. traveling _____

_____

4. insects _____

_____

5. packed _____

_____

Word Wise

| wings | insects | packed | tangled | traveling |

Rewrite each sentence. Use one of the words from the box in place of a word or phrase in the sentence.

1. Some animals with six legs build homes in the ground.

_____

2. The bird opened its parts that help it fly and flew away.

_____

3. The fire truck was going from one place to another to a fire.

_____

4. The horns of the goat got twisted in the fence.

_____

5. Tara filled up a suitcase when she spent the night with a friend.

_____

Writing

Write your own story about how you would catch a butterfly. Use as many words from the box as you can.

_____

_____

_____

_____

_____

Name _____   Date _____

A Family Hike

Read the story. Think about the meanings of the words in bold type.

My family likes to go **hiking**. We start **early** in the morning when the sun comes up. We fill our backpacks with water and food. Then, we put on **strong** shoes. My sister and I race to the top of the mountain. We like to see who will get there first. On the mountain, my family has a picnic. After we eat, Mom sits and looks at the beautiful sights. Dad and my sister go **exploring**. They look for rocks and animals. As for me, I **lean** back against a big rock and take a nap.

Look back at the words in bold type. Use clues in the story to figure out the meaning of each word. Write each word on the line next to its meaning.

_____ **1.** near the beginning

_____ **2.** looking in places that are new

_____ **3.** able to take heavy use

_____ **4.** to rest against someone or something

_____ **5.** taking a long walk

A Crossword Puzzle

Use the clues and the words in the box to complete the crossword puzzle.

| lean | early | strong | hiking | exploring |

Across
4. looking in places that are new

5. able to take heavy use

Down
1. near the beginning

2. to rest against

3. taking a long walk

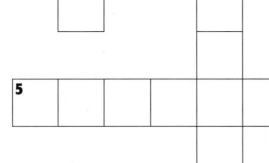

Word Wise

| lean | early | strong | hiking | exploring |

Choose the word from the box that makes sense in the sentences below.

1. Mom catches the train for work _____ in the morning.

2. When Nat goes _____, he walks as fast as he can up the trail.

3. Mrs. Carlos is _____ a cave that no one has ever been in.

4. Mikos needed a _____ box to carry the heavy books.

5. "Don't _____ against the wet paint on the wall!" Dad yelled.

Writing

Write your own story about a hiking trip. Use as many words from the box as you can.

_____

_____

_____

_____

_____

The Trip Alone

Read the story. Think about the meanings of the words in bold type.

Pedro was packing for a trip to his grandmother's house. He closed the last bag and put his **luggage** near the door. This would be his first trip alone on an airplane. He had been to many places, but a **journey** alone was something new. Pedro was excited.

When Pedro got on the plane, he started to feel scared. He was **nervous**. But everyone helped make Pedro feel **comfortable**. They gave him a pillow, food, and drinks. When the plane landed, it was time for Pedro to leave. He was sorry to say **farewell** to all the people on the airplane. But Pedro was very happy to see his grandmother!

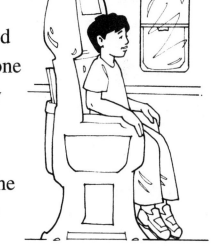

Look back at the words in bold type. Use clues in the story to figure out the meaning of each word. Write each word on the line next to its meaning.

_____ **1.** the suitcases and bags someone takes on a trip

_____ **2.** scared and worried; fearful

_____ **3.** good-bye

_____ **4.** a long trip

_____ **5.** feeling good; nothing hurts or is needed

Synonyms

A **synonym** is a word that has the same, or almost the same, meaning as another word.

EXAMPLES: start—begin   happy—glad

Choose the word from the box that matches its synonym. Write each word on the line.

> journey   nervous   luggage   farewell   comfortable

1. worried _____

2. feeling good _____

3. trip _____

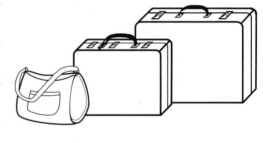

4. good-bye _____

5. suitcases _____

Dictionary Skills

 The words in a dictionary are listed in **ABC order**.

EXAMPLE: airplane, bag, pillow, trip

Write the words from the box above in ABC order. Write one word on each line.

1. _____

2. _____

3. _____

4. _____

5. _____

Name _____ Date _____

Word Wise

| journey   nervous   luggage   farewell   comfortable |

Choose the word from the box that makes sense in the sentences below.

1. Mrs. Jenkins carried her _____ off the airplane.

2. The _____ through the mountains would take several days.

3. Dad was so _____ that he did not want to get out of his chair.

4. Clara waved _____ before she got on the bus.

5. Juan was _____ and worried about the first day of school.

Writing

Write your own story about a trip you took by yourself. If you have not taken a trip alone, tell what you think it would be like to travel alone. Use as many words from the box as you can.

_____

_____

_____

_____

_____

A Shooting Star

Read the story. Think about the meanings of the words in bold type.

I wanted to see a shooting star. So one **summer** night, I went to visit my friend. She lives far from the lights of the city.

That night we lay on the grass and looked up at the sky. The **moon** was big and round. It looked like a **large**, yellow ball hanging in the dark sky. We could see clouds above, too. Sometimes, they would **float** in front of the moon. After watching for a long time, we finally saw a shooting star.

"Wow! Did you see that?" I asked my friend.

"That was **amazing**. I've never seen anything like it!" she said.

We sat quietly for a long time hoping to see another shooting star.

Look back at the words in bold type. Use clues in the story to figure out the meaning of each word. Write each word on the line next to its meaning.

_____ **1.** surprising

_____ **2.** big

_____ **3.** an object in the sky that moves around the Earth

_____ **4.** a season of the year that comes between spring and fall

_____ **5.** to move along slowly in the air

Word Groups

Words can be grouped by how they are alike.

EXAMPLE: places to live: city, town, farm

Read each group of words. Think about how they are alike. Write the word from the box that best completes each group.

moon	large	float	amazing	summer

1. interesting, surprising, _____

2. star, planet, _____

3. big, huge, _____

4. spring, winter, _____

5. move, swim, _____

Dictionary Skills

Guide words are two words at the top of each dictionary page. Guide words tell the first and last entry words on the page. All the words are in ABC order.

EXAMPLE: Guide words: **dark**   **long**

Entry words on page: far, hanging, lights

Darken the circle for the correct answer.

1. Which word would be between the guide words <u>back</u> and <u>gate</u>?

   Ⓐ float   Ⓑ amazing   Ⓒ large

2. Which word would be between the guide words <u>lip</u> and <u>road</u>?

   Ⓐ summer   Ⓑ moon   Ⓒ hoping

Word Wise

| moon | large | float | amazing | summer |

Choose the word from the box that makes sense in the sentences below.

1. Dad made a _____ pizza to feed five people.

2. We like to go swimming in the _____.

3. The _____ circles around the Earth.

4. Tran thinks it is _____ to watch bees build a hive.

5. The clouds _____ in the blue sky.

Writing

Write your own story about what it would be like to see a shooting star. Use as many words from the box as you can.

_____

_____

_____

_____

_____

_____

_____

Ralph Goes Camping

Read the story. Think about the meanings of the words in bold type.

"This looks like a good spot to camp," said Mr. Saenz. He parked the car. Ralph opened the door and **leaped** out. Mr. Saenz smiled as he watched Ralph jump around. Ralph couldn't help it. He was very excited. Ralph and his dad were going to sleep in a **tent**. They were going to catch fish and eat them for **dinner**.

"Can we go fishing first, Dad?" asked Ralph. "The **stream** is just down the hill. I can hear the water running."

"I guess the tent can wait," said Mr. Saenz with a **grin**. "Let's get the fishing poles and worms. I think it's time to catch some fish!"

Ralph smiled back at his dad. They were going to have the best trip ever.

Look back at the words in bold type. Use clues in the story to figure out the meaning of each word. Write each word on the line next to its meaning.

_____ **1.** the main food of the day, usually eaten at night; supper

_____ **2.** a kind of moving water

_____ **3.** a smile

_____ **4.** jumped

_____ **5.** a kind of house made of cloth or skin that is easily moved

Make a Picture

How do you picture words? Sometimes the picture you draw in your mind can help you remember the meanings of words.

Draw a picture for each of the words below.

EXAMPLE: pole	**3.** stream
1. grin	**4.** dinner
2. tent	**5.** leaped

Word Wise

| grin | tent | stream | leaped | dinner |

Choose the word from the box that makes sense in the sentences below.

1. Mr. West asked Jacob to set the table for _____.

2. Marcia and a friend slept in a _____ in the

backyard.

3. The baby gave his mother a big _____ when

he saw her.

4. The horse _____ over the fence.

5. Greg got wet when he fell into the _____.

Writing

Write your own story about a camping trip. Use as many words from the box as you can.

_____

_____

_____

_____

_____

_____

_____

Unit 3 Assessment

Darken the letter of the word that fits best in the sentence.

1. Mrs. Huang planted a garden in the ____.
Ⓐ bedroom
Ⓑ backyard
Ⓒ building

2. Dan built a ____ for his dog to sleep in.
Ⓐ barnyard
Ⓑ birdhouse
Ⓒ doghouse

3. Mom would not let us play ____ because it was raining.
Ⓐ outside
Ⓑ inside
Ⓒ anytime

4. Ted bought a large ____ to paint the house.
Ⓐ paintbrush
Ⓑ treetop
Ⓒ newspaper

5. A new ____ is moving in next door to us.
Ⓐ house
Ⓑ airplane
Ⓒ neighbor

6. The ____ barked at the bug.
Ⓐ kitten
Ⓑ puppy
Ⓒ piglet

7. Rita opened her ____ when it began to rain.
Ⓐ purse
Ⓑ raincoat
Ⓒ umbrella

8. Paul got a kitten that has soft and ____ fur.
Ⓐ fluffy
Ⓑ rough
Ⓒ hard

9. Miyoko likes to ____ to her grandmother sing.
Ⓐ whisper
Ⓑ listen
Ⓒ look

10. The cat ____ happily when Roberto pet it.
Ⓐ purred
Ⓑ laughed
Ⓒ squeaked

Unit 3 Assessment, page 2

Darken the letter of the word that fits best in the sentence.

11. Rick answered the phone when it ____.
- (A) sang
- (B) bang
- (C) rang

12. The clock in the hall ____ the hour.
- (A) chimed
- (B) spoke
- (C) heard

13. Lee ____ on the door, but no one was home.
- (A) ripped
- (B) knocked
- (C) answered

14. The dog stopped to ____ a tree.
- (A) sniff
- (B) thank
- (C) forget

15. Rick bought a name ____ for his dog to wear in case it got lost.
- (A) bowl
- (B) shirt
- (C) tag

16. The ____ swam to eat the bread we tossed into the water.
- (A) ducks
- (B) frogs
- (C) squirrels

17. Andy kept his toys high on a shelf where they were ____ from his little brother.
- (A) near
- (B) safe
- (C) helped

18. "Get your hand out of that cookie jar right now!" ____ Mother.
- (A) ordered
- (B) asked
- (C) laughed

19. Mr. West ____ picked up the hurt bird.
- (A) roughly
- (B) hardly
- (C) gently

20. The dog's ____ left muddy prints on the floor.
- (A) tail
- (B) shoes
- (C) paws

Skip's Doghouse

Read the story. Think about the meanings of the words in bold type.

Benny and his dad were sitting behind their house in the **backyard**. Benny's dad was reading the **newspaper**. Benny said, "Skip's **doghouse** is a mess! Would you help me fix it up?"

"Yes," said his dad. "We can paint the **outside**. It will look new."

Benny's dad went to the garage. He got a can of paint and a **paintbrush**.

"I think we have everything we need to paint Skip's doghouse," said Dad.

"Skip thinks we are missing something," said Benny.

Dad looked at Skip. Skip was holding the newspaper in his mouth. "I guess Skip does not want us to make a bigger mess," laughed Dad. "Maybe we should lay the newspaper on the ground so we don't get paint all over."

Look back at the words in bold type. Use clues in the story to figure out the meaning of each word. Write each word on the line next to its meaning.

_____ **1.** a paper with news that people read every day

_____ **2.** a small building for a dog

_____ **3.** something that is used to paint with

_____ **4.** the outer part of something

_____ **5.** a space behind a building

Compound Words

A **compound word** is a word formed by putting two or more words together.

EXAMPLES: playground = play + ground

birthday = birth + day

Read each compound word. Write the two words that make up the compound word. Then, use each compound word in a sentence.

1. doghouse _____

_____

2. outside _____

_____

3. paintbrush _____

_____

4. newspaper _____

_____

5. backyard_____

_____

Word Wise

| outside | doghouse | backyard | newspaper | paintbrush |

Rewrite each sentence. Use one of the words from the box in place of a word or words in the sentence.

1. Jesse used a big brush for paint to paint the fence.

_____

2. Mr. Sanders likes to read the paper with news written on it each morning.

_____

3. The dog dug a hole in the yard behind the house.

_____

4. Mrs. Sung washed the part that faces out of the window.

_____

5. Tia built a house for her dog.

_____

Writing

Write your own story about something you did for an animal. Use as many words from this lesson as you can.

_____

_____

_____

_____

Snowball

Read the story. Think about the meanings of the words in bold type.

Mrs. Reid lives next door. She is my **neighbor**. Mrs. Reid has a new **puppy** named Snowball. Snowball is white and **fluffy**. Mrs. Reid takes Snowball for a walk every day.

One day it was raining. Mrs. Reid did not want to go out in the rain. She called me and asked me to take Snowball for a walk. I got my raincoat and umbrella and went right over. Snowball was ready to go. I took her to the park. She ran so fast that I lost my **umbrella**.

"Slow down, Snowball!" I kept saying. But Snowball did not **listen**. She ran all around the park and all the way back home.

Look back at the words in bold type. Use clues in the story to figure out the meaning of each word. Write each word on the line next to its meaning.

_____ **1.** a person who lives nearby

_____ **2.** something that keeps the rain off

_____ **3.** a baby dog

_____ **4.** to try to hear

_____ **5.** soft

Analogies

An **analogy** compares words. It shows how the words are alike. An analogy has two parts. The two parts are joined by the word <u>as</u>.

EXAMPLE: <u>Wet</u> is to <u>rain</u> as <u>dry</u> is to <u>sun</u>.

Think about how the words in the first pair are alike. Write the word from the box to complete the analogy.

> **fluffy   listen   puppy   umbrella   neighbor**

1. <u>Television</u> is to <u>watch</u> as <u>radio</u> is to _____.

2. <u>Brick</u> is to <u>hard</u> as <u>pillow</u> is to _____.

3. <u>Cat</u> is to <u>kitten</u> as <u>dog</u> is to _____.

4. <u>Boy</u> is to <u>girl</u> as <u>enemy</u> is to _____.

5. <u>Snow</u> is to <u>mitten</u> as <u>rain</u> is to _____.

Dictionary Skills

The words in a dictionary are listed in **ABC order**.

EXAMPLE: home, park, rain, walk

Write words from the box above in ABC order. Write one word on each line.

1. _____

2. _____

3. _____

4. _____

5. _____

Word Wise

| fluffy | listen | puppy | umbrella | neighbor |

Choose the word from the box that makes sense in the sentences below.

1. Mara took her _____ because it looked

like it would rain.

2. Hua wanted to _____ to the radio.

3. The _____ barked at a bug.

4. Mother made a pie to take next door to our

_____ .

5. The baby sleeps with a soft and _____

blanket.

Writing

Write your own story about taking a puppy for a walk. Your story can be real or make-believe. Use as many words from the box as you can.

_____

_____

_____

_____

_____

_____

Too Much Noise!

Read the story. Think about the meanings of the words in bold type.

Lui sat in her bedroom and petted her cat, Sam. Sam **purred** softly. Lui's brother was gone. So the house was very quiet. Lui decide it was a good time to read. Just as she found a book, the telephone **rang**. Lui's mother answered the phone. Soon it was quiet again.

"Now I can read my book," Lui thought.

Before long, someone **knocked** on the door. Then, the dog **barked** loudly at the sound. Next, the big clock in the hall **chimed** the hour.

"Why is there so much noise now?" Lui asked.

Finally, just as things got quiet again, the front door opened. "I'm home!" her brother yelled.

Lui groaned. Now she would never be able to read.

Look back at the words in bold type. Use clues in the story to figure out the meaning of each word. Write each word on the line next to its meaning.

_____ **1.** a sound made by a happy cat

_____ **2.** a sound made by a telephone when someone calls

_____ **3.** a sound made by a dog

_____ **4.** a sound made by a big clock to tell the hour

_____ **5.** a sound made when something is hit

Sound Words

A word can name the sound something makes.

Write a sound word from the box beside each picture.

> rang   purred   barked   chimed   knocked

1.  _____

2.  _____

3.  _____

4.  _____

5. _____

Name _____   Date _____

Word Wise

| rang | purred | barked | chimed | knocked |

Choose the word from the box that makes sense in the sentences below.

1. Miguel answered the phone when it
_____.

2. The happy cat sat in the chair and _____.

3. A mail person _____ on the door and gave Mr. Hernandez a box.

4. The hall clock _____ each hour.

5. The dog _____ when the cat was in the tree.

Writing

Write your own story about noises in your home. Use as many words from the box as you can.

_____

_____

_____

_____

_____

_____

_____

_____

Rex and the Ducks

Read the story. Think about the meanings of the words in bold type.

Laura and her dog, Rex, walked along the **bank** of the river. Rex stopped to **sniff** the ground.

"What do you smell?" Laura asked.

Rex began to run down the path. His dog **tag** jingled as he ran. He kept sniffing the ground.

"Come back!" shouted Laura. She raced after Rex. When Laura found her dog, he was chasing some **ducks**. They ran to the water.

Laura laughed. "Those ducks are **safe** now! You don't like the water, Rex," she said.

Look back at the words in bold type. Use clues in the story to figure out the meaning of each word. Write each word on the line next to its meaning.

_____ **1.** to smell

_____ **2.** kinds of birds that can swim in water

_____ **3.** the ground beside a river or lake

_____ **4.** not in danger

_____ **5.** a label that is tied on

Multiple Meanings

Some words have more than one meaning. You can use clues in the sentence to tell which meaning the word has.

EXAMPLE: fish

meaning A: a group of animals that live in water. We eat fresh **fish** at the beach.

meaning B: to pull out. We had to **fish** the ring out of the sink drain.

Write the letter of the correct meaning next to each sentence.

bank

meaning A: the ground beside a river or lake

meaning B: a place for keeping money

_____ **1.** Mark fished from the bank of the lake.

_____ **2.** Sara put some money in the bank.

tag

meaning A: a label that is tied on

meaning B: a chasing game

_____ **3.** The children were playing tag.

_____ **4.** Tara pulled the price tag off the shirt she bought.

ducks

meaning A: kinds of birds that can swim in water

meaning B: bends down

_____ **5.** We saw the ducks on the lake.

_____ **6.** Lou ducks behind the tree so his sister cannot see him.

Word Wise

| tag | safe | bank | sniff | ducks |

Rewrite each sentence. Use one of the words from the box in place of a word or words in the sentence.

1. Irma read the label tied in the shirt before she washed it.

_____

2. The birds that can swim in water were looking for fish to eat.

_____

3. We pulled the boat onto the ground beside the lake.

_____

4. Pat likes to smell flowers that are sweet.

_____

5. The bird was not in danger from the cat when it was in the tree.

_____

Writing

Write your own story about what you like to do on a bank of a river or lake. Use as many words from the box as you can.

_____

_____

_____

_____

_____

Sit, Muffin!

Read the story. Think about the meanings of the words in bold type.

Beth went outside to find her puppy. Right away, Muffin began to jump up on her. Muffin's **paws** left muddy prints on Beth's shirt. "Get down, Muffin. It's time to teach you some **manners**!" Beth said.

"Sit, Muffin!" Beth **ordered**. Muffin just wagged his tail and looked at Beth.

"No, Muffin. You need to sit," Beth said again. Then, Beth **gently** pushed on Muffin's back. This time, Muffin sat.

"Good dog, Muffin," Beth said. She gave him some **treats** to help him know he did something special. Beth kept working with Muffin. He was a fast learner. Before long, Muffin would sit without a treat.

"What a good dog you are, Muffin!" Beth said. Muffin seemed to understand. He jumped up on Beth and gave her a big dog lick.

"Tomorrow you're going to learn not to jump!" Beth laughed.

Look back at the words in bold type. Use clues in the story to figure out the meaning of each word. Write each word on the line next to its meaning.

_____ **1.** things that are special

_____ **2.** ways to act

_____ **3.** told to do something

_____ **4.** the feet of some animals

_____ **5.** done in a kind way

Base Words

Base words are words without any endings or other word parts added to them. Some endings are **s**, **ed**, and **ly**. Sometimes the spelling of the base word changes when an ending is added to it.

EXAMPLES:

shirt	shirts
work	worked
wag	wagged
soft	softly

Write the base word of each word below.

1. ordered _____

2. gently _____

3. treats _____

4. manners _____

5. paws _____

Dictionary Skills

Guide words are two words at the top of each dictionary page. Guide words tell the first and last entry words on the page. All the words are in ABC order.

EXAMPLE: Guide words: **back   find**

Entry words on page: did, dog, fast

Darken the circle for the correct answer.

1. Which word would be between the guide words <u>long</u> and <u>need</u>?

   Ⓐ gently   Ⓑ learner   Ⓒ manners

2. Which word would be between the guide words <u>muddy</u> and <u>pushed</u>?

   Ⓐ ordered   Ⓑ treats   Ⓒ jumped

Word Wise

| paws | treats | gently | manners | ordered |

Use each word in the box to write new sentences.

1. _____

2. _____

3. _____

4. _____

5. _____

Writing

Write your own story about teaching a pet to do something. Use as many words from the box as you can.

_____

_____

_____

_____

_____

_____

_____

_____

_____

Unit 4 Assessment

Darken the letter of the word that means the same, or about the same, as the boldfaced word.

1. flowers in the **meadow**
- Ⓐ woods
- Ⓑ field
- Ⓒ basket

2. hang the **paintings**
- Ⓐ pictures
- Ⓑ frames
- Ⓒ clothes

3. fish in the **brook**
- Ⓐ large tank
- Ⓑ salty ocean
- Ⓒ small river

4. eating at a **restaurant**
- Ⓐ food place
- Ⓑ picnic table
- Ⓒ late time

5. look at **reptiles**
- Ⓐ books
- Ⓑ animals
- Ⓒ shoes

6. visit a **museum**
- Ⓐ building with special things
- Ⓑ an old friend
- Ⓒ place to shop

7. **difficult** to do
- Ⓐ fun
- Ⓑ easy
- Ⓒ hard

8. **teaching** how to cook
- Ⓐ watching
- Ⓑ helping learn
- Ⓒ thinking about

9. **remember** where it is
- Ⓐ show
- Ⓑ forget
- Ⓒ bring to mind

10. **wonderful** news
- Ⓐ sad
- Ⓑ great
- Ⓒ silly

Unit 4 Assessment, page 2

Darken the letter of the word that means the same, or about the same, as the boldfaced word.

11. walk **forward**
- Ⓐ to the back
- Ⓑ to the front
- Ⓒ to the side

12. a dress with **stripes**
- Ⓐ squares
- Ⓑ dots
- Ⓒ lines

13. join the **pieces**
- Ⓐ parts
- Ⓑ club
- Ⓒ fun

14. cut with **scissors**
- Ⓐ the teeth
- Ⓑ a sharp tool
- Ⓒ a wooden toy

15. blue **material**
- Ⓐ cloth
- Ⓑ house
- Ⓒ chair

16. **sew** a shirt
- Ⓐ join with thread
- Ⓑ clean with water
- Ⓒ look to buy

17. play with a **football**
- Ⓐ a ball that looks like a shoe
- Ⓑ a ball that looks like an oval
- Ⓒ a ball that looks like a foot

18. **everyone** is gone
- Ⓐ all people
- Ⓑ some people
- Ⓒ many people

19. ring the **doorbell**
- Ⓐ a bell that opens a door
- Ⓑ a bell with a door
- Ⓒ a bell outside a door

20. meet at the **playground**
- Ⓐ place to get dirt
- Ⓑ place to play
- Ⓒ place to grow flowers

My Father, the Artist

Read the story. Think about the meanings of the words in bold type.

My father is an artist. Every day he gets out his paints and brushes. He likes to paint pictures of the **meadow** behind our house. His **paintings** show the big field at different times of the year. My favorite painting shows the **season** of spring. I'm in the picture! Grandma was visiting us at that time. Grandma and I were sitting by the **brook splashing** our feet in the water. Father must have been watching. He made a beautiful picture of us. Father plans to give it to Grandma for her birthday.

Look back at the words in bold type. Use clues in the story to figure out the meaning of each word. Write each word on the line next to its meaning.

_____ **1.** pictures made with paint

_____ **2.** a flat, grassy place

_____ **3.** a time of year

_____ **4.** throwing water about

_____ **5.** a small river or stream

Word Puzzle

Write a word next to each meaning. Then, use the numbered letters to answer the question, "Who paints pictures?"

| brook | season | meadow | paintings | splashing |

1. a flat, grassy place ___ ___ ___ ___ ___ ___
                              1

2. a small river ___ ___ ___ ___ ___
                        2

3. pictures made with paint ___ ___ ___ ___ ___ ___ ___ ___ ___
                                            3

4. throwing water about ___ ___ ___ ___ ___ ___ ___ ___ ___
                                                    4

5. a time of year ___ ___ ___ ___ ___ ___
                            5

Answer: an ___ ___ ___ ___ ___ ___
           1   2   3   4   5   3

Word Wise

| brook   season   meadow   paintings   splashing |

Choose the word from the
box that makes sense in
the sentences below.

1. We hung our _____ on the wall to dry.

2. The dog was _____ in the water.

3. We caught fish in the _____.

4. The cows were eating grass in the _____.

5. Fall is my favorite _____ of the year.

Writing

Write your own story telling about a job someone in your family does.
Use as many words from the box as you can.

_____

_____

_____

_____

_____

_____

_____

Ming-Yen Comes to Visit

Read the story. Think about the meanings of the words in bold type.

Last **week** my cousin came to visit. Her name is Ming-Yen. I showed Ming-Yen all around the city. We went to the **museum** to see old bones. We went to a **restaurant** to eat. We went to the park to play. But our favorite place to visit was the zoo. Ming-Yen liked looking at the birds. But I liked the **reptiles** the best. I stayed in the reptile building for two **hours**. The people who cared for the snakes told me all about them. While I like looking at them, I don't think that I would like to hold one.

Look back at the words in bold type. Use clues in the story to figure out the meaning of each word. Write each word on the line next to its meaning.

_____ **1.** times that measure sixty minutes

_____ **2.** a place to eat

_____ **3.** a building where special things are kept and shown to visitors

_____ **4.** animals with dry skin that are covered in scales

_____ **5.** time that measures seven days

Word Web

Fill in the word web with words from the box.

week   hours   museum   reptiles   restaurant

Animal Word

_____

Ming-Yen Visits

Time Words

_____

_____

Place Words

_____

_____

Word Wise

week   hours   museum   reptiles   restaurant

Rewrite each sentence. Use one of the words from the box in place of a word or words in the sentence.

1. Allan likes to read books about animals with dry skin that are covered in scales.

_____

2. We got pizza at the place to eat.

_____

3. Our class took a trip to a building where special things are kept.

_____

4. Mr. Brooks took a trip that lasted for seven days.

_____

5. Gina and Mike were at the zoo for three times that measure sixty minutes.

_____

Writing

Write your own story about a time a family member came to visit. Use as many words from the box as you can.

_____

_____

_____

_____

_____

It's a Hit!

Read the story. Think about the meanings of the words in bold type.

Mr. Oliver and Rocky were playing ball in the park. Mr. Oliver was **teaching** his son how to hit a baseball.

"It is very **difficult** to hit the ball," said Rocky. "I just can't seem to swing the bat at the right time."

"I know that you can do it, Rocky!" said Mr. Oliver. "Just **remember** to keep your eyes on the ball."

Then, Mr. Oliver tossed the ball to Rocky. Rocky stepped **forward** and swung the bat. CRACK! The ball went flying into the air.

"I did it, Dad! I hit the ball," yelled Rocky.

"You did a **wonderful** job," answered Mr. Oliver. "I am so proud of you!"

Look back at the words in bold type. Use clues in the story to figure out the meaning of each word. Write each word on the line next to its meaning.

_____ **1.** toward the front

_____ **2.** to bring to mind

_____ **3.** hard

_____ **4.** very good

_____ **5.** helping a person learn

Antonyms

Antonyms are words that have opposite meanings.
EXAMPLES: happy—sad   quickly—slowly   small—large

Match the words in the box with their antonyms. Write each word on the line.

> forward   difficult   teaching   wonderful   remember

1. easy _____

2. terrible _____

3. backward _____

4. learning _____

5. forget _____

Dictionary Skills

The words in a dictionary are listed in **ABC order**.
EXAMPLE: home, park, rain, walk

Write words from the box above in ABC order. Write one word on each line.

1. _____

2. _____

3. _____

4. _____

5. _____

Word Wise

forward   difficult   teaching   wonderful   remember

Choose the word from the box that makes sense in the sentences below.

1. It was _____ for Maria to reach the jar on the top shelf.

2. Mrs. Thomas liked _____ the children in school.

3. The children faced _____ as they walked down the hall.

4. "Did you _____ to feed the dog?" asked Mother.

5. Paco and Greg had a _____ time playing games.

Writing

Write your own story about a time a family member helped you learn to do something. Use as many words from the box as you can.

_____

_____

_____

_____

_____

_____

Name _____ Date _____

Aunt Bea Sews

Read the story. Think about the meanings of the words in bold type.

My Aunt Bea likes to **sew**. I asked her to make a skirt for me. We went to a shop that sells **material**. We looked at all the cloth. I picked out one that had **stripes** on it. The lines were blue and purple. After Aunt Bea paid for it, we brought it home. Then, Aunt Bea started making the skirt. First, she used **scissors** to cut it out. Finally, she used a needle and thread to sew the **pieces** of the skirt together. When the skirt was done, I tried it on. It fit just right!

Look back at the words in bold type. Use clues in the story to figure out the meaning of each word. Write each word on the line next to its meaning.

_____ **1.** long, thin lines

_____ **2.** a tool that cuts

_____ **3.** make clothes with a needle and thread

_____ **4.** parts of something

_____ **5.** cloth

Analogies

An **analogy** compares words. It shows how the words are alike. An analogy has two parts. The two parts are joined by the word <u>as</u>.

EXAMPLE: <u>Wet</u> is to <u>rain</u> as <u>dry</u> is to <u>sun</u>.

Think about how the words in the first pair are alike. Write the word from the box to complete the analogy.

> sew   pieces   stripes   material   scissors

1. <u>Write</u> is to <u>pencil</u> as <u>cut</u> is to _____.

2. <u>Circles</u> are to <u>dots</u> as <u>lines</u> are to _____.

3. <u>House</u> is to <u>wood</u> as <u>skirt</u> is to _____.

4. <u>Bag</u> is to <u>sack</u> as <u>parts</u> is to _____.

5. <u>Hammer</u> is to <u>build</u> as <u>needle</u> is to _____.

Dictionary Skills

Guide words are two words at the top of each dictionary page. Guide words tell the first and last entry words on the page. All the words are in ABC order.

EXAMPLE: Guide words: **sale**   **started**

Entry words on page: sells, shop, skirt

Darken the circle for the correct answer.

1. Which word would be between the guide words <u>shape</u> and <u>sun</u>?

  Ⓐ scissors   Ⓑ sew   Ⓒ stripes

2. Which word would be between the guide words <u>pen</u> and <u>play</u>?

  Ⓐ pieces   Ⓑ purple   Ⓒ paid

Word Wise

sew	pieces	stripes	material	scissors

Choose the word from the box that makes sense in the sentences below.

1. Thomas cut the paper with _____.

2. The shirt had thin yellow _____ on it.

3. Mrs. Garza bought _____ to make a dress.

4. This puzzle has one hundred _____.

5. Bert got a needle and some thread to _____ a button on his coat.

Writing

What would you like to sew? Write your own story telling how you would do it. Use as many words from the box as you can.

_____

_____

_____

_____

_____

_____

_____

_____

_____

Happy Birthday, Uncle Ken!

Read the story. Think about the meanings of the words in bold type.

Randy looked out the window. "Here comes Uncle Ken. It is time for **everyone** to hide," he said.

When the **doorbell** rang, Randy opened the door. "Hello, Uncle Ken!" he said. "Come **inside** the house. I will go get my coat. Then, we can go to the **playground** to play ball."

As soon as Uncle Ken walked in the house, all of the family yelled, "Happy birthday!" Uncle Ken was so surprised that he dropped the **football** he was holding.

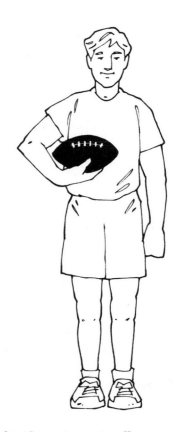

Look back at the words in bold type. Use clues in the story to figure out the meaning of each word. Write each word on the line next to its meaning.

_____ **1.** a bell that is by the outside of a door

_____ **2.** every person

_____ **3.** a place outside where people play

_____ **4.** a kind of ball that is an oval shape

_____ **5.** in or toward the part that is in

Compound Words

> A **compound word** is a word made by putting two or more words together.
>
> **EXAMPLES:** backpack, flashlight

Write compound words. Match one word from Box A with one word from Box B. Use each word only once. Write each new word in Box C.

Box A	Box B	Box C
play	side	1. _____
foot	one	2. _____
in	bell	3. _____
door	ball	4. _____
every	ground	5. _____

Write a sentence using each compound word in Box C.

1. _____

2. _____

3. _____

4. _____

5. _____

Word Wise

| inside | football | doorbell | everyone | playground |

Rewrite each sentence. Use one of the words from the box in place of a word or words in the sentence.

1. The children were playing soccer on the place where people play outside.

_____

2. Tia wants to invite every person in the class to her party.

_____

3. Jack bought a new brown oval ball.

_____

4. Mr. Parker answered the bell at the door when it rang.

_____

5. The kitten fell asleep in the part that is in the box.

_____

Writing

Write your own story telling about a surprise. Use as many words from the box as you can.

_____

_____

_____

_____

_____

Unit 5 Assessment

Darken the letter of the correct answer.

1. What is the prefix in the word unlocks?
   - Ⓐ un
   - Ⓑ lock
   - Ⓒ s

2. What is the prefix in the word replace?
   - Ⓐ re
   - Ⓑ rep
   - Ⓒ ace

3. What does the word refill mean?
   - Ⓐ do not fill
   - Ⓑ already full
   - Ⓒ fill again

4. What does the word unpack mean?
   - Ⓐ begin to pack
   - Ⓑ the opposite of pack
   - Ⓒ pack again

5. Which prefix makes underline{like} mean underline{not like}?
   - Ⓐ re
   - Ⓑ ed
   - Ⓒ un

6. Choose the word that correctly completes the sentence.
   Abe went ____ see the new puppy.
   - Ⓐ to
   - Ⓑ too
   - Ⓒ two

7. Choose the word that correctly completes the sentence.
   Can you ____ the bird singing?
   - Ⓐ here
   - Ⓑ her
   - Ⓒ hear

8. Choose the word that correctly completes the sentence.
   We went swimming in the ____.
   - Ⓐ seal
   - Ⓑ see
   - Ⓒ sea

9. Choose the word that correctly completes the sentence.
   Matt ____ a sandwich.
   - Ⓐ eight
   - Ⓑ ate
   - Ⓒ aid

Unit 5 Assessment, page 2

Darken the letter of the correct answer.

10. Which word has a suffix?

Ⓐ repaint

Ⓑ painter

Ⓒ paint

11. What is the suffix in the word <u>quickly</u>?

Ⓐ qu

Ⓑ ick

Ⓒ ly

12. What does the word <u>colorful</u> mean?

Ⓐ color again

Ⓑ full of color

Ⓒ one who colors

13. What does the word <u>neatly</u> mean?

Ⓐ done in a neat way

Ⓑ one who is neat

Ⓒ not neat

14. Which suffix can be added to the end of the word <u>work</u> to make a new word?

Ⓐ ly

Ⓑ er

Ⓒ ful

15. Choose the word that correctly completes the sentence.

Jan has ____ apples.

Ⓐ to

Ⓑ too

Ⓒ two

16. Choose the word that correctly completes the sentence.

An ____ has six legs.

Ⓐ and

Ⓑ ant

Ⓒ aunt

17. Choose the word that correctly completes the sentence.

Kim has a ____ shirt.

Ⓐ blue

Ⓑ boo

Ⓒ blew

18. Choose the Spanish word for the picture.

Ⓐ taco

Ⓑ burro

Ⓒ lasso

Name _____ Date _____

Prefixes

A **prefix** is a group of letters added to the beginning of a word. Adding a prefix to a word changes its meaning.
EXAMPLE:
Carla is **happy**.
Carla is **unhappy**.

Read the first sentence in each pair. Then, finish the second sentence. Add un to the word in dark type from the first sentence.

1. Max **locks** the box.

Margo _____ the box.

2. Max **sticks** a label to the box.

Margo _____ the label.

3. Max **ties** a string around the box.

Margo _____ the string.

4. Max **clips** two boxes together.

Margo _____ the boxes.

5. Max **loads** the boxes onto a truck.

Margo _____ the boxes.

More Prefixes

Remember that a **prefix** is a group of letters added to the beginning of a word. Adding a prefix to a word changes its meaning.

EXAMPLE: Julio **packs** his bag.

Julio **repacks** his bag. (Julio packs his back again.)

Prefix	Meaning	Example
re	again; back	rewrite
un	not; opposite	unwrap

Read the sentences. Underline each word that has a prefix. Tell the meaning of the word.

1. Sam wanted to refill his glass with juice. _____

2. Sam was unhappy because the jar was empty. _____

3. He was unable to find more juice. _____

4. Sam's mother returned from the store. _____

5. Sam helped his mother unpack the food. _____

6. Sam saw that his mother had a new jar of juice to replace the empty

one. _____

Prefixes in Context

Choose the word from the box that makes sense in the sentences below. Use each word one time only.

> unfair   returned   unhappy   unlike   unclear   redo

Mrs. Perez called Len to her desk. Mrs. Perez told Len that she could

not read his homework. The writing was

(1) _____. She asked Len to

(2) _____ the math problems. Len was

(3) _____ . He thought it was

(4) _____ he had to write the page again. But

Len was surprised to find that some of his answers were wrong. It was

(5) _____ him to miss any math problems.

So, Len was glad that he got to correct the homework. He

(6) _____ the page to Mrs. Perez the next day.

Writing

Write your own story about a time that you had to redo something. Use as many words with prefixes as you can.

_____

_____

_____

_____

_____

Suffixes

A **suffix** is a group of letters added to the end of a word. Adding a suffix to a word changes its meaning.

EXAMPLES: The suffix **ful** means "full of." hope**ful**, help**ful**

The suffix **ly** means "in a certain way." quick**ly**, sudden**ly**

Read each sentence. Choose one of the words below the line to complete the sentence. Write the word on the line.

1. The weaver worked _____.

                                       slow   slowly

2. He planned his rug _____.

                                  careful   carefully

3. He wanted a rug with a lot of _____.

                                      color   colorful

4. His friends paid a _____ visit to watch him work.

                                quick   quickly

5. They walked _____ by so they would not bother him.

                              quiet   quietly

6. The weaver was _____ when the rug was finished.

                              joy   joyful

More Suffixes

Remember that a **suffix** is a group of letters added to the end of a word.
Adding a suffix to a word changes its meaning.
EXAMPLE: The baby is **quiet**.
The baby plays **quietly**. (The baby plays in a way that is quiet.)

Suffix	Meaning	Example
er	one who	play<u>er</u>
ful	full of	help<u>ful</u>
ly	in a certain way	neat<u>ly</u>

Read the sentences. Underline each word that has a suffix from the box. Tell the meaning of the word.

1. Fernando is a painter.

_____

2. He lives in a beautiful rain forest.

_____

3. Fernando looks closely at everything he paints.

_____

4. Once he painted a playful monkey.

_____

5. The painting sold quickly.

_____

6. The person who bought it is a zoo worker.

_____

Suffixes in Context

Choose the word from the box that makes sense in the sentences below. Use each word one time only.

> helper   slowly   cheerful   gladly   teacher   colorful

Mr. Roland is our art **(1)** _____. He is

very **(2)** _____ and happy. He shows us

how to make many **(3)** _____ paintings.

He **(4)** _____ answers all our questions. Mr.

Roland wants us to work **(5)** _____ so we can do

our best work. We all take turns being his **(6)** _____.

Writing

Write your own story about a special teacher. Use as many words with suffixes as you can.

_____

_____

_____

_____

_____

_____

_____

Homophones

Homophones are words that sound the same but have different meanings. They usually have different spellings, too.

EXAMPLE: To means "in the direction of." Let's go **to** the mountains.

Too means "also." John will go, **too**.

Two means "one more than one." Meg has **two** dogs.

Read each sentence. Write <u>to</u>, <u>too</u>, or <u>two</u>.

1. Juan was going _____ the park.

2. His friend Jess was going, _____.

3. The _____ friends took a

baseball and bat.

4. Juan and Jess wanted _____ practice batting.

5. Juan and Jess saw Meg at the park, _____.

6. Meg wanted _____ play with them.

7. Meg had a baseball, _____.

8. The friends could not practice batting with

_____ balls.

9. So, Meg decided _____ put her ball down.

Homophones Practice

Homophones are words that sound the same but have different meanings. They usually have different spellings, too.

EXAMPLE:

rode   road

Read each sentence. Look at the pictures and the words below them. Write the word that makes sense.

1. I went to the beach with my

_____.

ant   aunt

2. The _____ was

very hot.

son   sun

3. We swam in the _____.

sea   see

4. Then, we _____ lunch.

eight   ate

5. I will _____ a letter

to thank her for a fun day.

write   right

Homophones in Context

Read each sentence. Choose one of the words below the line to complete the sentence. Write the word on the line.

Lena and her dad went for a walk in the woods. They turned

(1) _____ on the path. They climbed
     write   right

(2) _____ the top of a hill. Lena and her dad stopped
     to   too

and **(3)** _____ lunch there. An **(4)** _____
          ate   eight   ant   aunt

got on Lena's sandwich. Lena did not want **(5)** _____
                                                  two   to

share her food, so she pushed it off. Then, a raccoon came to visit,

(6) _____. It was so close that Lena could
     two   too

(7) _____ its black mask. The raccoon went
     sea   see

(8) _____ sleep by a tree. It was getting hot in the
     too   to

(9) _____. So, Lena
     son   sun

and her dad walked back down the path.

More Homophones

Homophones are words that sound the same but have different meanings. They usually have different spellings, too.

EXAMPLE:

Hear means "to listen to." We **hear** the bell ringing.

Here means "to this place" or "at this place." Bring the ball **here**.

Read each sentence. Write <u>hear</u> or <u>here</u>.

1. Did you _____ that the circus is coming?

2. Is it coming _____ soon?

3. Yes, it will be _____ today.

4. The parade will pass _____ soon.

5. I think I _____ the music now.

6. _____ it is!

7. Come over _____ and watch it with me.

8. Did you _____ the lions roar?

More Homophones Practice

Remember that **homophones** are words that sound the same but have different meanings. They usually have different spellings, too.

EXAMPLE: Rode means "sat on or in something to be carried."

Road means "a path used to go from one place to another."

The cowboy **rode** on the **road**.

Look at each pair of homophones. Then, use both homophones in a sentence. Draw a picture to go with each sentence.

1. not, knot

_____

_____

_____

2. knows, nose

_____

_____

_____

3. blew, blue

_____

_____

_____

4. for, four

_____

_____

_____

More Homophones in Context

Read each sentence. Choose one of the words below the line to complete the sentence. Write the word on the line.

The wind **(1)** _____ hard one day. Little Penguin
      blue   blew

watched the waves in the **(2)** _____. He decided
                    see   sea

(3) _____ go swimming. His friends did
      two   to

(4) _____ want to go with him. So, Little Penguin
      not   knot

jumped into the **(5)** _____ water alone.
            blue   blew

"I don't **(6)** _____ him," one penguin said.
        see   sea

"I will go look **(7)** _____ him."
              for   four

Soon a **(8)** _____ popped out of the water.
         nose   knows

"**(9)** _____ I am!" called Little Penguin.
   Here   Hear

Name _____ Date _____

Words from Spanish

Many English words come from other languages. One language is Spanish.

Read the words in the box. They are Spanish words that are used in English, too. Write each word below the picture it names.

burro	taco	lasso	fiesta	amigo	banana

1.

_____

4.

_____

2.

_____

5.

_____

3.

_____

6.

_____

Words from Other Languages

Many English words come from other languages.

Read the words in the box. They are words from other languages that are used in English, too. Write each word below the picture it names.

wig   cannon   hamburger   polka   piano   spaghetti

1.

_____

4.

_____

2.

_____

5.

_____

3.

_____

6.

_____

Name _____ Date _____

Clothing Words from Other Languages

The girl below is wearing clothing from different parts of the world. Read the list of clothing names that come from other languages. Then, fill in the labels on the picture.

Clothing	Description	Country
bandana	square of cloth	India
beret	small, flat hat	France
bolero	short vest	Spain
kimono	robe	Japan
moccasin	soft leather shoe	United States (Native American)
parka	hooded coat	Russia
skirt	covering that hangs from the waist	Scandinavia
sombrero	hat with wide brim	Spain
tote	carrying bag	Africa

Name _____ Date _____

Fun with Context Clues

Read the sentences. Use clues to guess what the words in dark print would mean if they were real words. Then, tell what clues helped you think as you do.

1. Roger helped his dad plant a **glonock**.

meaning: _____

clue: _____

2. He used a **tryglif** to dig the hole.

meaning: _____

clue: _____

3. Roger gave the plant some **flizzen** with a hose.

meaning: _____

clue: _____

4. Soon, a **crant** built a nest in it.

meaning: _____

clue: _____

Fun with Homograph Riddles

Homographs are words that have the same spelling but different
meanings. Sometimes homographs are said differently, too.
EXAMPLE: We **park** our car in the **park**.

**Read each riddle. Tell what the underlined word means in each riddle. Then,
write a sentence to show a different meaning for each underlined word.**

1. Question: Why did the farmer call his pig Ink?

Answer: because it kept running out of the <u>pen</u>

meaning: _____

sentence: _____

2. Question: When is a piece of wood like a king?

Answer: when it's a <u>ruler</u>

meaning: _____

sentence: _____

Vocabulary Skills, Grade 2, Answer Key

pages 4–5
1. C, 2. B, 3. C, 4. A, 5. C,
6. A, 7. B, 8. A, 9. C, 10. B,
11. C, 12. C, 13. A, 14. C,
15. A, 16. C, 17. A, 18. B,
19. C

pages 6–7
1. B, 2. C, 3. A, 4. B, 5. A,
6. C, 7. A, 8. C, 9. A, 10. B,
11. C, 12. A, 13. B, 14. B,
15. C, 16. B, 17. C, 18. B,
19. C, 20. A

pages 8–9
1. B, 2. A, 3. C, 4. A, 5. B,
6. C, 7. A, 8. C, 9. A, 10. B,
11. C, 12. B, 13. A, 14. A,
15. C, 16. B, 17. C, 18. A,
19. A, 20. C

page 10
1. frowned, 2. brave,
3. rainy, 4. downstairs,
5. enemies

page 11
Antonyms:
1. enemies, 2. frowned,
3. brave, 4. rainy,
5. downstairs
Dictionary Skills:
1. brave, 2. downstairs,
3. enemies 4. frowned,
5. rainy

page 12
1. rainy, 2. frowned,
3. brave, 4. downstairs,
5. enemies

page 13
1. shoot, 2. swing,
3. basket, 4. court, 5. watch

page 14
1. B, 2. A, 3. A, 4. B, 5. B,
6. A

page 15
Sentences may vary.
1. Mr. Edwards carefully
   pushed the baby on the
   swing.
2. The players will meet at
   the court after school.
3. The crowd yelled happily
   when the ball went into
   the basket.
4. Ed and Meiko come to
   the park to shoot the
   basketball.
5. Jay bought a new watch
   so that he would never be
   late again.

page 16
1. giggle, 2. fortunate,
3. frighten, 4. behave,
5. foolish

page 17
Synonyms:
1. D, 2. E, 3. C, 4. A, 5. B
Dictionary Skills:
1. A, 2. C

page 18
1. fortunate, 2. giggle,
3. behave, 4. foolish,
5. frighten

page 19
1. awful, 2. chalk,
3. sidewalk, 4. broke,
5. wondered

page 20
Word Groups:
1. broke, 2. chalk,
3. sidewalk, 4. awful,
5. wondered
Dictionary Skills:
1. awful, 2. broke, 3. chalk,
4. sidewalk, 5. wondered

page 21
1. wondered, 2. sidewalk,
3. chalk, 4. broke, 5. awful

page 22
1. wasn't, 2. I've, 3. isn't,
4. don't, 5. couldn't

page 23
Sentences will vary.
1. isn't, 2. couldn't, 3. I've,
4. don't, 5. wasn't

page 24
Sentences may vary.
1. The boys don't want to
   go to the park.
2. Dana couldn't wait to eat
   dinner.
3. I've read that book
   already.
4. Pam isn't going to ride
   the bus today.
5. The dog wasn't in the
   backyard.

pages 25–26
1. A, 2. C, 3. B, 4. A, 5. C,
6. B, 7. A, 8. B, 9. A, 10. C,
11. C, 12. A, 13. C, 14. B,
15. B, 16. A, 17. C, 18. C,
19. A, 20. C

page 27
1. traveling, 2. tangled,
3. packed, 4. wings,
5. insects

page 28
Sentences will vary.
1. wing, 2. tangle, 3. travel,
4. insect, 5. pack

page 29
Sentences may vary.
1. Some insects build
   homes in the ground.
2. The bird opened its
   wings and flew away.
3. The fire truck was
   traveling to a fire.
4. The horns of the goat got
   tangled in the fence.
5. Tara packed a suitcase
   when she spent the night
   with a friend.

page 30
1. early, 2. exploring,
3. strong, 4. lean, 5. hiking

page 31
Across: 4. exploring,
5. strong
Down: 1. early, 2. lean,
3. hiking

page 32
1. early, 2. hiking,
3. exploring, 4. strong,
5. lean

page 33
1. luggage, 2. nervous,
3. farewell, 4. journey,
5. comfortable

page 34
Synonyms:
1. nervous, 2. comfortable,
3. journey, 4. farewell,
5. luggage
Dictionary Skills:
1. comfortable, 2. farewell,
3. journey, 4. luggage,
5. nervous

page 35
1. luggage, 2. journey,
3. comfortable, 4. farewell,
5. nervous

page 36
1. amazing, 2. large,
3. moon, 4. summer,
5. float

page 37
Word Groups:
1. amazing, 2. moon,
3. large, 4. summer, 5. float
Dictionary Skills:
1. A, 2. B

page 38
1. large, 2. summer,
3. moon, 4. amazing 5. float

page 39
1. dinner, 2. stream, 3. grin,
4. leaped, 5. tent

page 40
Answers may vary.

page 41
1. dinner, 2. tent, 3. grin,
4. leaped, 5. stream

pages 42–43
1. B, 2. C, 3. A, 4. A, 5. C,
6. B, 7. C, 8. A, 9. B, 10. A,
11. C, 12. A, 13. B, 14. A,
15. C, 16. A, 17. B, 18. A,
19. C, 20. C

page 44
1. newspaper, 2. doghouse,
3. paintbrush, 4. outside,
5. backyard

page 45
Sentences will vary.
1. dog+house, 2. out+side,
3. paint+brush,
4. news+paper,
5. back+yard

page 46
Sentences may vary.
1. Jesse used a big paintbrush
   to paint the fence.
2. Mr. Sanders likes to read
   the newspaper each
   morning.
3. The dog dug a hole in the
   backyard.
4. Mrs. Sung washed the
   outside of the window.
5. Tia built a doghouse.

page 47
1. neighbor, 2. umbrella,
3. puppy, 4. listen, 5. fluffy

page 48
Analogies:
1. listen, 2. fluffy, 3. puppy,
4. neighbor, 5. umbrella
Dictionary Skills:
1. fluffy, 2. listen,
3. neighbor, 4. puppy,
5. umbrella

page 49
1. umbrella, 2. listen,
3. puppy, 4. neighbor,
5. fluffy

page 50
1. purred, 2. rang,
3. barked, 4. chimed,
5. knocked

page 51
1. barked, 2. chimed,
3. knocked, 4. purred,
5. rang

page 52
1. rang, 2. purred,
3. knocked, 4. chimed,
5. barked

page 53
1. sniff, 2. ducks, 3. bank,
4. safe, 5. tag

page 54
1. A, 2. B, 3. B, 4. A, 5. A,
6. B

page 55
Sentences may vary.
1. Irma read the tag in the
   shirt before she washed it.
2. The ducks were looking
   for fish to eat.
3. We pulled the boat onto
   the bank.
4. Pat likes to sniff flowers
   that are sweet.
5. The bird was safe from
   the cat when it was in the
   tree.

page 56
1. treats, 2. manners,
3. ordered, 4. paws,
5. gently

page 57
Base Words:
1. order, 2. gentle, 3. treat,
4. manner, 5. paw
Dictionary Skills:
1. C, 2. A

page 58
Sentences will vary.

pages 59–60
1. B, 2. A, 3. C, 4. A, 5. B,
6. A, 7. C, 8. B, 9. C, 10. B,
11. B, 12. C, 13. A, 14. B,
15. A, 16. A, 17. B, 18. A,
19. C, 20. B

page 61
1. paintings, 2. meadow,
3. season, 4. splashing,
5. brook

page 62
1. meadow, 2. brook,
3. painting, 4. splashing,
5. season
Answer: an artist

page 63
1. paintings, 2. splashing,
3. brook, 4. meadow,
5. season

page 64
1. hours, 2. restaurant,
3. museum, 4. reptiles,
5. week

page 65
Animal Word: reptiles
Time Words: week, hours
Place Words: museum,
restaurant

page 66
Sentences may vary.
1. Allan likes to read books
   about reptiles.
2. We got pizza at the
   restaurant.
3. Our class took a trip to a
   museum.
4. Mr. Brooks took a trip
   that lasted for a week.
5. Gina and Mike were at
   the zoo for three hours.

page 67
1. forward, 2. remember,
3. difficult, 4. wonderful,
5. teaching

page 68
Antonyms:
1. difficult, 2. wonderful,
3. forward, 4. teaching,
5. remember
Dictionary Skills:
1. difficult, 2. forward,
3. remember, 4. teaching,
5. wonderful

page 69
1. difficult, 2. teaching,
3. forward, 4. remember,
5. wonderful

page 70
1. stripes, 2. scissors,
3. sew, 4. pieces,
5. material

page 71
Analogies:
1. scissors, 2. stripes,
3. material, 4. pieces,
5. sew
Dictionary Skills:
1. C, 2. A

page 72
1. scissors, 2. stripes,
3. material, 4. pieces, 5. sew

page 73
1. doorbell, 2. everyone,
3. playground, 4. football,
5. inside

page 74
Answer order may vary.
Sentences will vary.
playground; football; inside;
doorbell; everyone

page 75
Sentences may vary.
1. The children were
   playing soccer on the
   playground.
2. Tia wants to invite
   everyone in the class to
   her party.
3. Jack bought a new
   football.
4. Mr. Parker answered the
   doorbell when it rang.
5. The kitten fell asleep
   inside the box.

pages 76–77
1. A, 2. A, 3. C, 4. B, 5. C,
6. A, 7. C, 8. C, 9. B, 10. B,
11. C, 12. B, 13. A, 14. B,
15. C, 16. B, 17. A, 18. C

page 78
1. unlocks, 2. unsticks,
3. unties, 4. unclips,
5. unloads

page 79
Answers may vary.
1. refill; fill again,
2. unhappy; not happy,
3. unable; not able,
4. returned; came back
again, 5. unpack; opposite
of pack, 6. replace; fill the
place again

page 80
1. unclear, 2. redo,
3. unhappy, 4. unfair,
5. unlike, 6. returned

page 81
1. slowly, 2. carefully,
3. color, 4. quick, 5. quietly,
6. joyful

page 82
1. painter; one who paints,
2. beautiful; full of beauty,
3. closely; in a way that is
close, 4. playful; full of
play, 5. quickly; in a way
that is quick, 6. worker; one
who works

page 83
Answers may vary.
1. teacher, 2. cheerful,
3. colorful, 4. gladly,
5. slowly, 6. helper

page 84
1. to, 2. too, 3. two, 4. to,
5. too, 6. to, 7. too, 8. two,
9. to

page 85
1. aunt, 2. sun, 3. sea,
4. ate, 5. write

page 86
1. right, 2. to, 3. ate, 4. ant,
5. to, 6. too, 7. see, 8. to,
9. sun

page 87
1. hear, 2. here, 3. here,
4. here, 5. hear, 6. Here,
7. here, 8. hear

page 88
Sentences will vary.

page 89
1. blew, 2. sea, 3. to, 4. not,
5. blue, 6. see, 7. for,
8. nose, 9. Here

page 90
1. amigo, 2. burro, 3. fiesta,
4. lasso, 5. banana, 6. taco

page 91
1. piano, 2. canon,
3. spaghetti, 4. hamburger,
5. wig, 6. polka

page 92
beret—hat;
bandana—bandana;
bolero—vest;
kimono—dress;
skirt—skirt; tote—purse;
moccasins—shoes

page 93
Answers will vary.

page 94
Answers will vary.
1. underlined meaning: a
place to keep animals;
another meaning: a writing
tool, 2. underlined meaning:
a measuring tool; another
meaning: a ruler of a
country